US Heavy Cruisers

in action

Part 2

By Al Adcock

Color by Don Greer

Illustrated by Andrew Probert

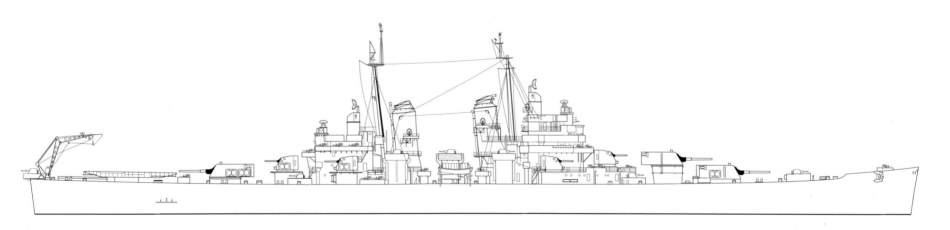

Warships Number 15

squadron/signal publications

The USS BALTIMORE (CA-68) fires her anti-aircraft guns at Japanese aircraft attacking the heavy cruiser off Luzon in the Philippines in mid-December of 1944. The BALTIMORE was operating with the 3rd Fleet in support of US efforts to liberate the Philippines from Japanese control. The name ship of her class, the BALTIMORE was the only heavy cruiser camouflaged in Measure 32/16D. This scheme consisted of Haze Gray (5-H, FS35237), Ocean Gray (5-O, FS35164), and Navy Blue (5-N, FS35044).

Acknowledgements

All photographs used in this publication are from official US Navy sources and have been declassified and supplied by the following photo archivists:

George Chizmar, Real War Photos, Hammond, Indiana (realwarphotos@yahoo.com)
Tom Walkowiak, Floating Drydock, Kresgeville, Pennsylvania (http://floatingdrydock.com)
Bob Carlisle, Elsilrac Enterprises, Winter Haven, Florida (elsilrac@earthlink.net)

Other photographs for this book were supplied by:
Andrew Probert
US Navy via Glen Phillips

I would like to thank all of them for their help in compiling the photographs and other information provided by the five gentlemen. Their help is greatly appreciated.

I also wish to thank Robert Nazak and Larry L. Bond for their help with this book.

ISBN 0-89747-431-7

If you have any photographs of aircraft, armor, soldiers or ships of any nation, particularly wartime snapshots, why not share them with us and help make Squadron/Signal's books all the more interesting and complete in the future. Any photograph sent to us will be copied and the original returned. The donor will be fully credited for any photos used. Please send them to:

Squadron/Signal Publications, Inc.
1115 Crowley Drive
Carrollton, TX 75011-5010

Если у вас есть фотографии самолётов, вооружения, солдат или кораблей любой страны, особенно, снимки времён войны, поделитесь с нами и помогите сделать новые книги издательства Эскадрон/Сигнал ещё интереснее. Мы переснимем ваши фотографии и вернём оригиналы. Имена приславших снимки будут сопровождать все опубликованные фотографии. Пожалуйста, присылайте фотографии по адресу:

Squadron/Signal Publications, Inc.
1115 Crowley Drive
Carrollton, TX 75011-5010

軍用機、装甲車両、兵士、軍艦などの写真を所持しておられる方はいらっしゃいませんか？どの国のものでも結構です。作戦中に撮影されたものが特に良いのです。Squadron/Signal社の出版する刊行物において、このような写真は内容を一層充実し、興味深くすることができます。当方にお送り頂いた写真は、複写の後お返しいたします。出版物中に写真を使用した場合は、必ず提供者のお名前を明記させて頂きます。お写真は下記にご送付ください。

Squadron/Signal Publications, Inc.
1115 Crowley Drive
Carrollton, TX 75011-5010

The USS BALTIMORE sails in the Pacific Ocean on 14 April 1944 in the company of a NEW ORLEANS class heavy cruiser. The BALTIMORE is camouflaged in Measure 21, an overall Navy Blue scheme. Two Vought OS2U Kingfishers are positioned on the catapults. (Real War Photos)

Introduction

The role of the US heavy cruiser was fully defined during World War Two when most of the US Pacific Fleet was severely damaged at Pearl Harbor, Hawaii on 7 December 1941. No heavy cruiser was damaged and all were able to carry the fight to the Japanese (and Germans) once the war plans were revised.

Sail and steam powered the first cruisers; the sails for range and the steam for speed. By the early 1900s, the sails were deleted and naval architects began to employ modern hull shapes. Wood gave way to steel in the hulls, and more powerful rifled guns became available. This increase in firepower necessitated the need for additional armor plating. The result was two types of warships: armored and protected. The armored cruiser had an armored deck, while the protected cruiser had both side and deck armor. All of the additional weight resulted in a requirement for more powerful engines. Some protected cruisers had up to 20 boilers to provide steam for the turbines or reciprocating engines.

The US Navy's first all steel protected cruisers were the **ATLANTA** and **BOSTON**. Both ships were constructed using the finest materials available at the time. The two cruisers were commissioned in the 1880s and went on to serve with distinction in the US Navy. The ATLANTA was scrapped in the 1912, while the BOSTON — renamed **DISPATCH** — continued to serve through World War Two as a receiving ship until she was sunk as an artificial reef in 1946.

Several types of cruisers have served with the US Navy from armored to protected, 1st, 2nd and 3rd class cruisers and battle cruisers to light, heavy and large cruisers. The light and heavy cruiser designation was determined by various naval treaties agreed upon in Washington and London following World War One. The governments of the United Kingdom, United States, Japan, France, and Italy agreed on various limits to the displacements and gun sizes of battleships and cruisers. The cruisers were placed into two categories: light cruisers were limited to 10,000 tons (9072 MT) displacement and 6-inch (15.2 CM) guns, while heavy cruisers were limited to 10,000 tons and 8 inch (20.3 CM) guns. When the US Navy began the construction of the first of the 'treaty' heavy cruisers[1], the PENSACOLA class actually came in 1000 tons (907.2 MT) under the treaty limit of 10,000 tons displacement, putting them at a disadvantage as far as armor protection was concerned.

The last US heavy cruiser built under the limits of the treaty was the **WICHITA** and she was laid down on the builder's ways in 1935. When the Germans attacked Poland in September of 1939, the treaty became void and the world's major navies began the design and construction of larger and heavier armored and armed cruisers and battleships. The **BALTIMORE/OREGON CITY** and **ALASKA** class cruisers were the direct result of no treaty limits on displacement, armor, or gun power.

The main armament of the WICHITA and BALTIMORE class heavy cruisers was the 8-inch/55 caliber[2] naval rifle firing a 260 pound (117.9 KG) projectile at muzzle velocity of 2800 feet (853.4 M) per second. The gun's range amounted to some 31,700 yards (28,986.5 M). The ALASKA class was armed with 12-inch/50 caliber guns firing a 1140 pound (517.1 KG) projectile out to 36,800 yards (33,649.9 M). The WICHITA's secondary battery consisted of 5-inch/38 guns in both single open and enclosed mounts. The BALTIMORE and ALASKA class cruisers employed 5-inch/38 guns in enclosed twin mounts. These dual-purpose guns, used mainly for anti-aircraft protection, had an altitude range of 37,200 feet (11,338.6 M) when fired at an 85° angle. The maximum range against surface targets amounted to 18,200 yards (16,642.1 M) when fired at a 45° angle. Close in antiaircraft protection was provided by 20MM Oerlikon and 40MM Bofors automatic cannon. Both were licensed produced in the US since the Oerlikon was a Swiss design, while the Bofors weapon originated in Sweden. The 1.1-inch (28MM) quad automatic gun, dubbed the 'Chicago Piano' was originally installed in the WICHITA and was planned for installation in the BALTIMORE class, however, its complexity and excessive maintenance problems caused its withdrawal from service. The WICHITA was also armed early in its career with the water-cooled 0.50 caliber (12.7MM) machine gun. These weapons were soon replaced by the more powerful and longer ranging 20MM cannon.

[1] See US Heavy Cruisers in Action, Part 1 (4014), squadron/signal publications, 2001.

[2] The caliber of a naval gun is the barrel's length divided by the bore diameter. For example, the 8-inch/55 caliber gun had a barrel length of approximately 440 inches (1117.6 CM), divided by the 8-inch bore to arrive at 55 caliber.

The NEWARK (C-1) was the first US Navy ship classified by hull number as a cruiser. The NEWARK was built by Cramp and Sons, Philadelphia and launched on 19 March 1890. Displacing 4083 tons (3704.1 MT) and armed with 12 6-inch guns, the NEWARK was armored with up to three inches of deck armor. (Real War Photos)

The BALTIMORE (CA-3) served in World War One as a minelayer. She displaced 4413 tons (4003.5 MT) and was armed with four 8-inch/35 and six 6-inch/30 guns mounted in barbettes on the side of the deck. The BALTIMORE was built by Union Iron Works, San Francisco and launched on 19 July 1888. All of her sail equipment was removed by the early 1900s. The deck is covered with air intakes for the boiler rooms. (Real War Photos)

Radar and other electronic gear was fitted to heavy cruisers as early as 1939 when the **CHICAGO** (CA-29) had a CXAM air-search radar set installed. The WICHITA and BALTIMORE classes benefited from the early research and development and were fitted with the latest radar sets available. The usual sets were the SG surface search (one on the main mast and one on the foremast) and an SK 'bedspring' air-search antenna on the fore mast. Most sailors on the cruisers had no idea what the antennas were for, since they were considered secret. IFF (Identification Friend/Foe) antennas began appearing in 1944 and they transmitted or received signals from other ships and aircraft to determine their identity. By 1945, some of the BALTIMORE/OREGON CITY class cruisers were being fitted with improved SK-2 and SG-2 sets with increased range.

World War One (WWI) saw the first, large scale employment of camouflage on warships. The camouflage schemes were designed to confuse an observer as to the ship's type, class, speed, distance and shape. Much study was undertaken by the Royal Navy, and to a lesser extent the US Navy, in regards to the effectiveness of ship camouflage. Nevertheless, both navies employed camouflage, mainly on destroyers and cargo ships during WWI — an effort to conceal convoys and their escorts from roaming German U-boats (submarines). The period between the wars saw little activity in the use of camouflage. Most US Navy ships were simply painted light or dark gray at the whim of the area commander. The onset of World War Two revived the study and implementation of camouflage schemes; some resembling WWI schemes. In 1942, the WICHITA was camouflaged in Measure 12, a scheme that employed both Sea Blue (FS35045) and Ocean Gray (FS35164). When the early BALTIMORE class cruisers began leaving the shipyards, they were usually camouflaged in Measure 21, an overall Navy Blue (FS35044) scheme. Measure 21 was found to be ineffective against aerial observations, leading to the introduction of the Measure 22 scheme. Measure 22 was a 'graded' system consisting of Navy Blue and Haze Gray (FS35237). Measure 21 was mainly employed in the Pacific and Measure 22 in the Atlantic; however, there were exceptions to this rule. Some cruisers were painted in multi-color 'dazzle' patterns, which were intended to confuse the ship's size and shape in the enemy's eyes.

The heavy cruisers were fitted with two catapults and one or two aircraft handling cranes. The WICHITA and BALTIMORE classes each had their catapults and cranes mounted on the quarterdeck/fantail, while the ALASKA class had theirs fitted amidships — a reversion to the earlier position of the 'treaty' cruisers. Aircraft types consisted of the Curtiss **SOC/SON Seagull**, Vought **OS2U/OS2N Kingfisher**, and the Curtiss **SC-1 Seahawk**. These aircraft types varied from ship to ship and according to the time frame. In general, the Seagull was carried early in the war, the Kingfisher during the mid war period, and the Seahawk by late 1944 and early 1945. The cruisers' aircraft were assigned to Cruiser Scouting Squadrons (VCS) with two to four aircraft per ship. Aircraft were used to spot naval gunfire, perform liaison duties, and conduct search and rescue (SAR) missions.

US Navy heavy cruisers were named for US cities, with one exception: the **USS CANBERRA** (CA-70), named to honor the Australian cruiser HMAS CANBERRA. The cruiser was lost with the US heavy cruisers **ASTORIA** (CA-34), **VINCENNES** (CA-44), and **QUINCY** (CA-39) during the Battle of Savo Island on 9 August 1942. Today, US nuclear attack submarines (SSN) are named for US cities.

US ships were awarded Battle Stars for their flag when they participated in a particular naval campaign, such as the Battle of Coral Sea, the Battle of Midway, or the Battle of the Philippine Sea. The USS WICHITA was the most highly decorated of the late heavy cruisers, earning 13 Battle Stars for her service in both the Atlantic and Pacific Theatres. The most highly decorated of all the later heavy cruisers was the **USS ST PAUL** (CA-73); she earned 17 Battle Stars for her combined service during World War Two, Korea, and Vietnam.

The WICHITA, BALTIMORE/OREGON CITY and the ALASKA class cruisers compiled an exemplary service record during World War Two, earning a total of 52 Battle Stars between them. Eleven of the BALTIMORE class were in commission before the war in the Pacific ended with more still on the builders ways. The three classes contributed to the final defeat of the Japanese Navy and Empire in the Pacific.

The armored cruiser PITTSBURGH (CA-4) was originally named the PENNSYLVANIA (ACR-4), but that name was reallocated to the new battleship PENNSYLVANIA (BB-38) that was launched on 16 March 1915. The PITTSBURGH was used by Eugene Ely to make the first aircraft landing on a ship. The PITTSBURGH was armed with four 8-inch/40 guns paired in deck gunhouses, 14 6-inch/50 guns, and 18 3-inch/50 weapons. Smaller weapons were used for anti-aircraft defense. (Real War Photos)

The RALEIGH (CA-8) was built by Norfolk Navy Yard and launched on 31 March 1892. She was armed with a single 6-inch/40 gun, ten 5-inch/40, eight 6-pounders, two 1-pounders, and four 18-inch torpedo tubes at the waterline. During the 1899-1902 time frame, the torpedo tubes were removed and an additional two boilers were added. The sails, originally fitted as a means of backing up the main propulsion system (and in some respects as a fuel saving device), were also removed to reduce top weight. (Real War Photos)

Development

WICHITA Class

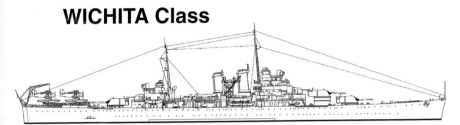

BALTIMORE Class

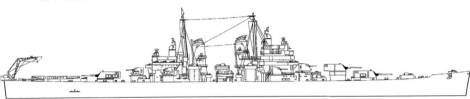

OREGON CITY Class

ALASKA Class

BOSTON Class (CAG)

ALBANY
Class (CG)

NORTHAMPTON Class (CC)

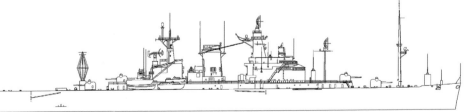

WICHITA Class

The WICHITA (CA-45) was the only ship in her class. She was built under a provision in the 1930 London Naval Treaty, which allowed the US to build one heavy cruiser in 1935. She was named for a large city in Kansas.

The WICHITA was laid down by the Philadelphia Navy Yard on 28 October 1935 and launched on 16 November 1937. After her trials, fitting out, and some additional yard time, the WICHITA was commissioned on 16 February 1939.

The cruiser was basically an 8-inch (20.3 CM) gunned **BROOKLYN** (CL-40) class light cruiser with upgrades to her anti-aircraft defenses and some machinery modifications. She was 600 feet (182.9 M) long at the waterline, while her overall length amounted to 608 feet 4 inches (185.4 M). Her beam was 61 feet 9 inches (18.8 M). She displaced 10,590 tons (9607 MT) standard and 13,015 tons (11,807 MT) full war load. The cruiser had a draught of 23 feet 9 inches (7.24 M) at full load.

The WICHITA's power came from eight Babcock and Wilcox boilers operating at 648° Fahrenheit (342.2° C) and a pressure of 464 pounds per square inch (3199.3 kPa). Over 100,000 horsepower was available to the four Parsons geared turbines that drove the four screws. Speed at full power was rated 33 knots (61.2 KMH). Her oil bunkers contained 1995 tons (1809.9 MT) of fuel oil — sufficient for a range of some 10,000 nautical miles (18,288 KM) at 15 knots (27.8 KMH). A pair of diesel electric generators were installed to provide additional electric power for the electronic gear and to act as a backup power supply in the event of a loss of steam power to the geared electric turbines.

The heavy cruiser's main side armor belt — protecting the magazines and engineering spaces — ranged from 4.5 to 6.5 inches (11.4 to 16.5 CM). Deck armor amounted to 2.25 inches (5.7 CM), while the barbettes were protected by 7 inches (17.8 CM) of armor. The turrets were faced with 8 inches (20.3 CM), with 2.27 inches (5.8 CM) on the roof and 3.37 inches (8.5 CM) on the sides. The conning tower was encircled with 6 inches (15.24 CM) of armor.

The WICHITA was armed with nine 8-inch/55 caliber Mk 12 Mod 1 guns. Three guns were mounted in each of the three turrets — two forward and one aft. Each turret, with guns, weighed 314 long tons (351.7 tons/319 MT). The guns fired a 260 pound (117.9 KG) projectile at a muzzle velocity of 2800 feet (853.4 M) per second. The weapon's range amounted to some 31,700 yards (28,986.5 M). The 8-inch guns were originally directed by the optical Mk 34 director. In 1943, this director was provided with radar to improve its effectiveness. Each turret was also equipped with a back-up optical range finder.

Secondary armament was originally scheduled to have been the 5-inch (12.7 CM)/25 caliber dual-purpose guns in single mounts, however the more effective 5-inch/38-caliber guns were installed when these became available. Initially only six of the eight guns were installed due to concerns over top heaviness. Four of the six 5-inch guns were enclosed in single gunhouses; the remaining two guns were placed in open mounts amidships. Following trials and additional testing, the last two 5-inch open mounts were installed in late 1939.

Additional anti-aircraft protection was provided by eight 0.50-inch (0.50 caliber/12.7MM)

(Above) The WICHITA (CA-45) sits in a drydock at the Philadelphia Navy Yard on 16 March 1939. The WICHITA was constructed at the Philadelphia Navy Yard and launched on 16 November 1937. Her paint scheme is Measure 3, the Light Gray (FS36320) System. A black boot topping separates the gray upper hull and red oxide lower hull. The red oxide coating helped to prevent — or at least slow — the buildup of speed robbing barnacles and other marine life on the hull. (Floating Drydock)

(Right) With her time in drydock over, the WICHITA leaves the Philadelphia Navy Yard on 11 August 1939 to conduct a shakedown cruise to the Caribbean. Less than one month later, she reported for service with Cruiser Division Seven (CruDiv-7) following the outbreak of World War Two in Europe. (Floating Drydock)

The WICHITA served with the Neutrality Patrol in the Atlantic protecting US shipping interests in 1940. Her number one and two turrets have what was believed to be a red stripe painted fore-and-aft, while the number three turret had a blue dot to identify her as being a US warship. She now carries her full armament of nine 8-inch guns in three turrets, eight 5-inch/38 dual-purpose guns — four in single mount enclosed gun houses and four in open mounts — and eight 0.50 caliber water-cooled machine guns in single mounts. A large searchlight tower was mounted between the funnels. (Real War Photos)

The WICHITA rides at hard anchor following her collision with the merchantman WEST NOHNO in Hvalfjordur Harbor, Iceland on 10 January 1942 during a severe storm. The WICHITA eventually grounded doing some minor damage to her hull and stem that required repairs at New York Navy Yard. She is camouflaged in Measure 12 with splotches. (Real War Photos)

water-cooled machine guns installed around the bridge area. In 1941 the WICHITA was armed with two quad-mounted 1.1-inch (28MM) anti-aircraft guns. These weapons were soon removed in favor of the far more effective 40MM Bofors cannons. By 1945, her defensive anti-aircraft armament consisted of four quad 40MM mounts, four twin 40MM mounts, and 18 20MM Oerlikon cannons in single mounts.

The WICHITA was fitted with two catapults: one mounted on each side of the quarterdeck. The catapult used a black powder charge to launch the aircraft. A single aircraft-handling crane was placed on the fantail's centerline. The multi-role crane was used to handle the ship's aircraft, boats, and cargo. An aircraft hangar, covered by a single horizontal sliding hatch, was set between the Number Three turret and the stern. The hangar had a capacity for four Curtiss SOC float biplanes with their wings folded. WICHITA originally embarked the Curtiss SOC Seagull, a float equipped scout biplane that initially saw service on the cruiser with Cruiser Scouting Squadron Seven (VCS-7). The Vought OS2U Kingfisher replaced the SOC in 1943. In 1945, the Curtiss SC-1 Seahawk, a single seat scout floatplane, briefly saw service before the Pacific War ended.

The WICHITA sailed to North Africa to support the upcoming Operation TORCH landings in North Africa in November of 1942. While engaging Vichy French naval vessels off Casablanca, Morocco, the WICHITA was hit by a 194MM (7.6 in) shell fired from a shore battery at El Hank. The round hit the WICHITA's port side just below the main mast, entered the second deck, and detonated in the crew quarters. The resulting explosion wounded 14 crewmembers — none seriously — and started fires that were quickly extinguished by damage control parties. Although she remained fully operational, the WICHITA returned to the United States for repairs after four days in combat.

Once her repairs were completed, the WICHITA sailed for the Pacific war zone. She arrived in time for the battle off Rennell Island in the Solomons on 29 January 1943. The older heavy cruiser USS CHICAGO (CA-29) was lost due to multiple aerial torpedo hits, while the WICHITA absorbed a single torpedo, which failed to detonate. The following year, the WICHITA was credited with aiding in the sinking of the Japanese aircraft carrier **CHIYODA** and the destroyer **HATSUZUKI** during the extended Battle of Leyte Gulf in October of 1944.

The WICHITA was also involved in the fighting around Okinawa and the final capitulation of Japan in 1945. While off Okinawa on 27 April 1945, she was struck by a small caliber round — believed to be a 5-inch projectile — fired from a Japanese shore battery. The round hit the port side just below the waterline and slightly aft of the Number Three turret. The explosion caused minor flooding, but the WICHITA continued in full operation.

The WICHITA served on active duty with the US Navy from February 1939 to February 1947 when she placed in the Atlantic Reserve Fleet. She was struck from the Navy list and sold for scrap in 1959. Her active duty career saw her serve in both the Atlantic and Pacific where she earned 13 Battle Stars.

(Above) The WICHITA sails off the port quarter of the British cruiser HMS EDINBURGH on their way to British naval anchorage at Scapa Flow, Scotland on 3 April 1942. The WICHITA was assigned to Task Force 39, which conducted training with the British Home Fleet for a month and then escorted North Atlantic convoys from Russia to Iceland. (Real War Photos)

(Below) The WICHITA is fired upon by the French battleship JEAN BART off Casablanca during Operation TORCH — the Allied invasion of northwest Africa on 8 November 1942. The guns of the JEAN BART were soon silenced by accurate fire from both the WICHITA and the battleship MASSACHUSETTS (BB-59). An ensuing exchange of gunfire from French shore batteries resulted in a hit on the port side of WICHITA that wounded 14 sailors. (Real War Photos)

(Above) The WICHITA and the carrier USS WASP (CV-7) lie at anchor at Scapa Flow in the Orkney Islands north of Scotland in April of 1942. The WASP and WICHITA are both camouflaged in Measure 12 with splotches. The stern mounted aircraft-handling crane is hoisting aboard a Curtiss SOC scout plane from Cruiser Scouting Squadron Seven (VCS-7). The WASP ferried Supermarine Spitfires to Malta on two occasions. (Real War Photos)

An aerial view of the WICHITA reveals the open aircraft hangar door and the below deck hangar space in January of 1943. The hangar had a capacity of four Curtiss SOC Seagull scout aircraft with the wings folded. Two single mount 20MM Oerlikon cannons were added to either side of the fantail. Splinter shields were erected around the deck mounted 5-inch/38 dual-purpose guns. (Floating Drydock)

In contrast to previous heavy cruisers, the WICHITA mounted her aircraft handling crane, hangar door, and catapults on the fantail. The watertight hangar door slid forward on tracks to allow access to the hanger bay below. The catapults employed a gunpowder charge to bring a SOC to flying speed in their 60-foot (18.3 M) length. The catapults rotated 360˚ to turn the aircraft into the wind. (Floating Drydock)

In February of 1944, the WICHITA became the Flagship for Cruiser Division Six (CruDiv-6) in the Pacific. She was now camouflaged in Measure 22, the Graded System. Three of her Curtiss SOC scout planes are on the catapults. An SG sea search radar antenna has been mounted half way up the foremast. The jack – a blue flag with 48 white stars – flew from the jackstaff on her bow. (Floating Drydock)

The open mount port side 5-inch/38 crews man their guns off Guam in May of 1944. Further aft, the twin mount 40MM Bofors cannons await at the ready and the 8-inch guns are trained toward the shore. The guns soon opened up on Japanese shore batteries inflicting heavy casualties. The WICHITA and the NEW ORLEANS (CA-32) are credited with sinking the Japanese carrier CHIYODA following fierce aerial attacks by US Naval Aviation forces off Samar and the WICHITA with the sinking of Japanese destroyer HATSUZUKI. (Real War Photos)

The WICHITA's main armament consisted of nine 8-inch/55 naval rifles mounted in three turrets, two forward and one aft. The 8-inch guns had a range of 31,700 yards (18 miles/29 KM) when firing a 260-pound armor piercing (AP) round. The barrels of the guns are fitted with a tampion to keep out water and foreign objects such as birds. The forecastle deck was steel, while the main deck was steel covered with teak wood. (Floating Drydock)

.50 Caliber (12.7MM) Water-Cooled Machine Gun

5 Inch (12.7 CM)/38 Caliber Gun, Open Mount

5 Inch/38 Caliber Gun, Enclosed Mount

Mk 34 Gun Director

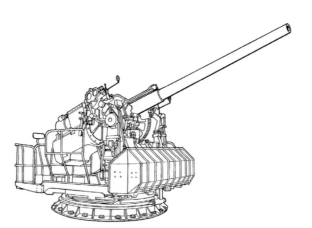

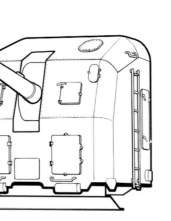

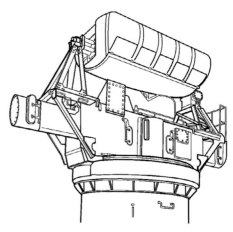

BALTIMORE Class

The BALTIMORE class heavy cruisers became the standard by which all later heavy 'gun' cruisers would be judged — both during and after the Second World War. These ships traced their lineage back to the earlier and successful WICHITA class heavy cruiser and BROOKLYN class light cruisers.

The class leader BALTIMORE (CA-68) was ordered on 1 July 1940 and laid down at Bethlehem Steel, Fore River, Quincy, Massachusetts on 26 May 1941. The first eight of the BALTIMORE class (CA 68-75) were built at Quincy. When the OREGON CITY (CA-122) was laid down, she was separated from her BALTIMORE class sisters into a new class due to a design change. The OREGON CITY class cruisers consisted of the lead ship, the **ALBANY** (CA-123) and the **ROCHESTER** (CA-124). These ships were also constructed by Bethlehem Steel. The OREGON CITY class were single stack ships, while the earlier BALTIMORE class cruisers had two stacks. The class was further divided in 1950 when the **DES MOINES** (CA-134) was designated the leader of a class of three ships – DES MOINES, **SALEM** (CA-139) and **NEWPORT NEWS** (CA-148) – to again separate them from their earlier sisters due to major configuration changes.

The BALTIMORE/OREGON CITY class heavy cruisers were 673 feet 6 inches (205.3 M) in overall length, 664 feet (202.4 M) at the waterline, and had a beam of 70 feet 10 inches (21.6 M) . Displacement was rated at 14,472 tons (13,129 MT) standard and 17,030 tons (15,450 MT) fully war loaded. At their full war load, the ships drew 26 feet 10 inches (8.2 M) of water. The

The BALTIMORE (CA-68) was the lead ship in a new class of heavy cruisers constructed without the burden of the Washington Naval Treaty. Commissioned on 15 April 1943, the BALTIMORE served with the 3rd and 5th Fleet in the Pacific providing fire support to amphibious landings and screening the fleet carriers from air attacks. SG sea-search radars have been mounted atop her main and foremasts, while the 'bedspring' SK air-search radar antenna is on her main mast. (Real War Photos)

later DES MOINES class grew to 716 feet 6 inches (218.4 M) in length and a beam of 76 feet 6 inches (23.3 M). The additional length and beam resulted in an increased displacement of 17,000 tons (15,422 MT) standard and 21,500 tons (19,505 MT) fully loaded.

All three of the classes were powered by eight Babcock and Wilcox boilers producing steam for the four General Electric geared turbines. The boiler and engine rooms were staggered to prevent one damaged engineering space from completely disabling the ship. A total of 120,000 horsepower was available to turn the four screws and speed was rated at 33 knots (61.2 KMH). Their range on internal fuel oil was rated at 10,000 nautical miles (18,531.3 KM) at 15 knots (27.8 KMH), however, this could be extended by underway replenishment.

The armor on the BALTIMORE class was similar to the earlier WICHITA class in that the hull sides were protected with plating that tapered from 6 inches (15.24 CM) over the machinery spaces to 4 inches (10.2 cm) at the waterline. The deck was armored with 2 inches (5 CM) and had 6 inches around the main gun barbettes. The turrets were faced with 8 inch (20.3 CM) armor plate and had 3 inches (7.62 CM) on the roof and 3 inches on the sides. The conning tower was allotted 8 inches of armor protection.

The BALTIMORE/OREGON CITY cruisers were armed with nine 8-inch (20.3 CM)/55 caliber Mk 12 or Mk 15 guns divided into three turrets. Like the earlier WICHITAs, the BALTIMOREs mounted two turrets forward and one aft. The guns had a range of 30,000 yards (27,432 M) when firing a 335-pound (151.9 KG) armor piercing (AP) round. The DES MOINES class was armed with nine of the automatic 8-inch/55 Mk 16 Mod 0 guns — again, three per turret. The new, and heavier, 8-inch gun had a rate of fire of 12 rounds per minute firing cased ammunition versus the earlier separate round/bagged ammunition. Main battery fire control consisted of the Mk 34 gun director which employed both optical and radar ranging.

The cruiser's secondary armament consisted of twelve 5-inch (12.7 CM)/38 caliber dual-purpose guns in six twin-mount gunhouses. Fire control was accomplished via the Mk 37 director using optical and radar ranging. The Mk 37 was used against aerial and surface targets. Anti-aircraft defenses consisted of the well-proven 40MM Bofors cannon. The first four of the

WICHITA Class

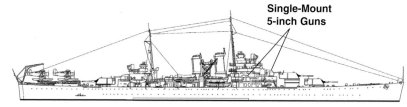

Single-Mount 5-inch Guns

BALTIMORE Class

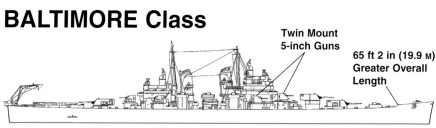

Twin Mount 5-inch Guns

65 ft 2 in (19.9 M) Greater Overall Length

BALTIMORES (CA 68-71) were armed with twelve quad mounts, for a total of 48 40MM gun barrels. The remaining ships were armed with 11 quad mounts and a pair of twin mounts on the fantail. The twin mounts came about when the two aft mounted aircraft handling cranes were replaced by a single centerline mounted unit. Twenty-four 20MM Oerlikon cannons were fitted over the course of the war. Following the war, the 40MM and 20MM guns were removed and automatic 3-inch (7.62 CM) guns were installed, with much reduced barrels.

Like the earlier WICHITA, the BALTIMORE class was fitted with an aircraft hangar and a pair of aircraft handling cranes in CA 68-71. A single crane was fitted to the remaining ships in the class. The OREGON CITY/DES MOINES classes were all fitted with a single crane on the fantail centerline. All of the classes were fitted with two catapults on the quarterdeck. Three types of scout floatplanes were embarked: the Curtiss SOC Seagull initially, followed by the Vought OS2U Kingfisher in 1943, and the Curtiss SC-1 in 1945. The end of the war in the Pacific prevented all of the ships having their floatplanes replaced by the SC-1.

By the time the BALTIMORE class heavy cruisers arrived in the Pacific and Atlantic war zones, the desperate defensive battles of early 1942 were a thing of the past. The initial Allied offensives and the violent cruiser and destroyer actions of late 1942 and early 1943 were also at an end. The Imperial Japanese Navy's carrier force and, perhaps just as importantly, its cadre of experience aircrew, was a shadow of its former self. With the large scale surface actions waning, the BALTIMORE class heavy cruisers were used to screen the fast carrier task forces punching holes in the shrinking defensive ring around Japan. The heavy cruisers were also used in the shore bombardment role from the Marshall Islands to Okinawa and the Japanese home islands.

The CANBERRA (CA-70) was struck on her starboard side by a single, deep running Japanese aerial torpedo on 13 October 1944. The torpedo hit between the number three and four fire rooms, rupturing the bulkhead and flooding both compartments. The explosion also displaced the outboard propeller shaft, tearing open the bulkhead and flooding the adjacent engine rooms. Both the explosion and flooding resulted in severe machinery damage and the loss of all power. CANBERRA was towed to a repair facility at Manus in the Admiralty

Islands. She was undergoing repairs during the last months of the war in the Pacific.

The **PITTSBURGH** (CA-72) was the only other BALTIMORE class cruiser to suffer any large scale damage during World War Two — and that came at the hands of Mother Nature. On 4 June 1945, shortly after her participation in the Okinawa campaign, the PITTSBURGH rode out a typhoon. The wind and wave action proved strong enough to rip the entire bow section off the ship. A transverse bulkhead just forward of the Number One turret prevented further flooding and the heavy cruiser arrived in Guam for temporary repairs. The severed bow — still floating — was also found and towed to Guam as well. The bow section, dubbed McKeesport for a suburb of Pittsburgh, was not grafted back onto the ship. The PITTSBURGH was repaired in the US, but did not participate further in the conflict.

Most of the BALTIMORE class heavy cruisers operated in the Pacific. Only the **QUINCY** (CA-71)[1] spent any appreciable time in the Atlantic. She first took part in the Normandy landings on 6 June 1944, providing fire support for the US assault on Utah Beach. She then moved to the Mediterranean, where she provided fire support for the landings in southern France. By late February of 1945, the need for QUINCY's presence in the Mediterranean Sea had lessened considerably. She was sent to the Pacific for the upcoming Okinawa campaign.

By the end of the war, eleven BALTIMORE class heavy cruisers were in commission with seven of them earning Battle Stars for their actions. The ST PAUL (CA-73) was the most highly decorated of the BALTIMORE class earning one Battle Star in World War Two, eight in Korea, and eight for her service in Vietnam. A total of 34 Battle Stars were earned by all of the BALTIMORE class in World War Two.

[1] Named for the USS QUINCY (CA-39) sunk at Savo Island on 9 August 1942.

The BALTIMORE class cruisers were armed with nine 8-inch guns in three turrets and twelve 5-inch/38 dual-purpose guns in six gunhouses. Two OS2U Kingfisher observation floatplanes are spotted on the catapults. A 40MM quad mount is positioned between the two aircraft handling cranes. In August of 1944, the BALTIMORE was called upon to transport President Franklin D. Roosevelt on an inspection tour of Pearl Harbor, Hawaii and Alaska. (Real War Photos)

BALTIMORE Class

Two Exhaust Funnels

OREGON CITY Class

One Exhaust Funnel

13

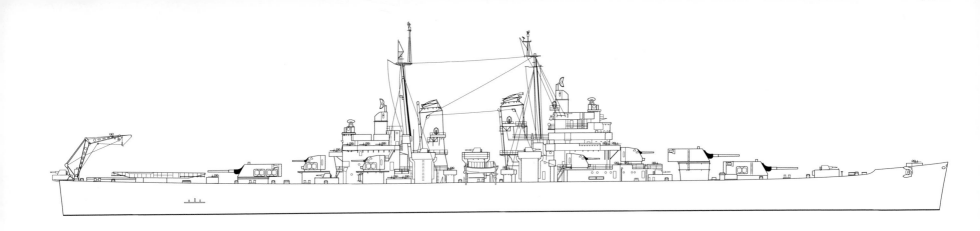

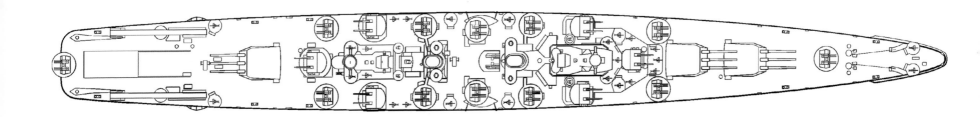

USS BALTIMORE (CA-68) Specifications

Length: 673 feet 6 inches (205.2 M)
Beam: 70 feet 10 inches (21.6 M)
Draft: 26 Feet 10 Inches (8.2 M)
Displacement: 14,472 Tons (13,129 MT) Standard, 17,030 Tons (15,450 MT) Full Load
Propulsion: 120,000 HP/Four Screws
Speed: 33 Knots (61.2 KMH)

Compliment: 1700 Officers and Men
Armament: 9 x 8-Inch (20.3 CM)/55 Guns in Triple Turrets, 12 x 5-Inch (12.7 CM)/38 Guns in Twin Turrets, 48 x 40MM Bofors Cannon in Quad Mounts, 24 x 20MM Oerlikon Cannon in Single Mounts
Aircraft: 4 SOC, OS2U, or SC Floatplanes

The BALTIMORE cruises at speed in the open Pacific in 1943. Her guns pointed in different directions and her aircraft handling cranes were lowered across the quarterdeck. The two 5-inch/38 guns in the port forward gunhouse are raised to maximum elevation — 85°. These weapons had an altitude range of 37,200 feet (11,338.6 M) when fired at maximum elevation. When used against surface targets, the 5-inch gun had a maximum range of 18,200 yards (16,642.1 M) when fired at a 45° angle. The ship was painted in Measure 21, the overall Navy Blue (FS35044) scheme. A small white pennant number (68) was painted on the BALTIMORE's bow. (Elsilrac)

The BALTIMORE at sea with two Vought OS2U-3 Kingfishers from VCS-10 on the catapults in 1944. The BALTIMORE was built by Bethlehem Steel Company in Quincy, Massachusetts and launched on 28 July 1942. The aft Mk 37 5-inch director is guiding the number six 5-inch mount. Judging by her wake, the BALTIMORE appears to be making approximately 25 knots (46.3 KMH) in the open Pacific. (Floating Drydock)

In 1944, the BALTIMORE was camouflaged in Measure 32/16d, the only ship in her class to be so painted. A pair of OS2U Kingfisher scout aircraft are situated on the catapults. BALTIMORE fought from Makin Island to Japan during her career in the Pacific, earning herself nine Battle Stars in the process. (Elsilrac)

15

The BOSTON (CA-69) in Boston Harbor on the day of her commissioning, 30 June 1943. She is riding high in the water, above the black boot topping. Her bunkers were soon filled with oil and she was fully supplied for her journey through the Panama Canal and into the Pacific. In the Pacific, the cruiser joined with Task Force 58, the fast fleet carrier force. The BOSTON was painted in Measure 21, the overall Navy Blue Scheme that was deemed to be effective against *kamikaze* (suicide aircraft) attacks. (Floating Drydock)

The BOSTON is maneuvered by a LCM (Landing Craft, Medium) in preparation for her being put in a floating drydock in November of 1944, following a year of fighting in the Pacific. Her Navy Blue paint scheme shows a great deal of wear from exposure to the salty Pacific Ocean. The BOSTON is just returning from raids on Luzon Island, in the Philippines. (Floating Drydock)

The BOSTON served with Task Forces 38 and 58 (TF 38 and 58) for her entire service in the Pacific during 1944. TF 38 was the fleet carrier force under 3rd Fleet command, while the same force was TF 58 when assigned to the 5th Fleet. On 29 October 1944, the BOSTON sailed from the Battle of Leyte Gulf, Philippines Islands to raid Luzon Island. She was the second BALTIMORE class ship and was constructed by Bethlehem Steel at Quincy, Massachusetts. She was launched on 26 August 1942. (Floating Drydock)

The BOSTON enters the floating drydock for some much-needed painting and overhaul in 1944. Once she was in position and properly chocked, the water was pumped out, exposing the BOSTON's hull for cleaning and painting. The BOSTON was part of the fast carrier Task Force 58 that was destined to attack the Japanese home islands. The Mk 34 main gun director mounted above the bridge lacked the antenna cover applied to some directors. (Real War Photos)

Mk 34 Main Gun Director (With Cover)

Mk 34 Main Gun Director (Without Cover)

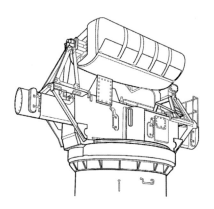

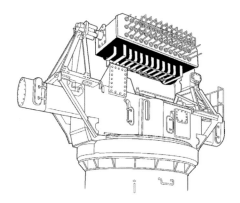

The BOSTON takes water over the bow while crewmen take some measure of cover behind the forward 40MM quad mount. The Number One and Two 8-inch turrets are trained to approximately 45° to starboard. The barrels of the 8-inch guns are covered to prevent the intrusion of seawater into the bore. The four round objects on each turret roof were vents designed to remove gun gases from the turret interior. A periscope for use by the turret crew jutted out from the aft starboard turret roof. (Floating Drydock)

The CANBERRA (CA-70, ex-PITTS-BURGH) was the only US Navy ship to be named for a foreign city during World War Two. She was named to honor the Royal Australian Navy cruiser HMAS CANBERRA, which was named for Australia's capital city. The HMAS CANBERRA was lost along with the older heavy cruisers ASTORIA (CA-34), QUINCY (CA-39) and VINCENNES (CA-44) during the Battle of Savo Island on 9 August 1942. The CANBERRA was launched from Bethlehem Steel Company, Quincy Massachusetts on 19 April 1943. She is riding high in the water, due to her lightly loaded condition. Following her commissioning on 14 October 1943, the heavy cruiser joined the Pacific Fleet's Task Force 58. (Floating Drydock)

The CANBERRA is barely underway following her commissioning in October of 1943. She was camouflaged in Measure 21, the overall Navy Blue System. The black boot topping immediately above the waterline protected the ship's side from spilled oil in the water. She carries an SG sea-search radar atop her main and foremast. The standard SK air-search radar antenna was either not fitted to the main mast or it was painted out by wartime censors. The CANBERRA and three of her sisters – BALTIMORE (CA-68), BOSTON (CA-69), and the later QUINCY (CA-71) – had two aircraft handling cranes mounted on the fantail. The remaining ships in their class had only one crane fitted. (Floating Drydock)

The CANBERRA is taken under-tow by the WICHITA off Formosa on 15 October 1944 after being hit by a Japanese aerial torpedo. The torpedo hit just below the armor belt in the area of the after fire room. Before damage control efforts became effective, the engineering compartments became flooded — stopping the ship. She was towed to Manus for temporary repairs before she could sail to the US for permanent repairs. (Real War Photos)

Mk 37 Director for the 5 Inch (12.7 CM) Guns

5 Inch Mk 12 Gunhouse

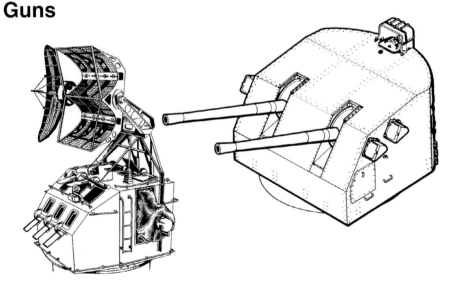

The CANBERRA enters a floating drydock (ARD) in Ulithi, Micronesia in December of 1944 to repair the damage caused by a Japanese aerial torpedo. The damage was found to be too great for permanent repair in the field forcing the ship back to the US. She carries an SG surface search and an SK air search radar atop her foremast. (Floating Drydock)

Once towed to Manus, the CANBERRA was placed in a drydock for temporary repairs. The torpedo hit killed 23 crewmen, blew a hole in the hull and seriously damaged the surrounding hull plates, frames, and bulkheads. Permanent repairs at Boston Navy Yard took eight months. The CANBERRA was still in the repair yard when the Pacific war ended, denying her any measure of revenge. (Real War Photos)

The QUINCY (CA-71) leaves Boston Harbor on the day of her commissioning — 15 December 1943. She was named for the earlier heavy cruiser QUINCY (CA-39), which was sunk at the Battle of Savo Island in 1942. She carries Measure 21, the Navy Blue (FS35044) System, above her boot topping. The quad 40MM mount between the twin aircraft handling cranes, as well as other, 40MM mounts, is covered to protect it from the weather. The QUINCY later sailed for the Gulf of Paria, between Trinidad and Venezuela, for her shakedown cruise before reporting for duty in the Atlantic Fleet. (Floating Drydock)

The QUINCY prepares to sail for the Caribbean Sea to conduct her shakedown cruise. The cruise lasted until she was assigned to Task Force 22 for training out of Casco Bay, Maine. She then reported to Task Group 27.10 for duty in Europe. Her recently painted Measure 32/18d camouflage already shows some wear and tear below the Number two turret — perhaps from a wharf strike. Measure 32/18d was used to counter German U-boats operating in the Atlantic. (Floating Drydock)

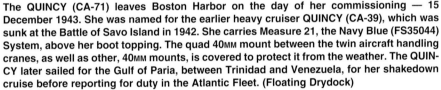

The QUINCY cruises in the open Atlantic in late May of 1944, just before the June invasion of Europe. She carries two Vought OS2U Kingfisher scout aircraft on her catapults. The Kingfishers spotted gunfire for the cruiser's 8-inch guns, which fired upon the beaches and inshore targets of Utah Beach. The Number Eight quad 40MM mount was located between the two aircraft handling cranes on the fantail. The QUINCY's Measure 32/18d camouflage consisted of Light Gray (FS36320), Ocean Gray (FS35164), and Dull Black (FS37040). (Floating Drydock)

The QUINCY displays her camouflage Measure 32/18d in May of 1944. The QUINCY, like most of the wartime heavy cruisers, was built in the Bethlehem Steel Shipyard in Quincy, Massachusetts. She was launched on 23 June 1943 and commissioned on 15 December 1943. Once completed, she sailed to Europe for duty with the 12th Fleet. She participated in the invasion of Europe on 6 June 1944, conducting shore bombardment on Utah Beach. (Floating Drydock)

Two Vought OS2U Kingfishers of VCS-10 are spotted on the QUINCY's catapults in May of 1944. Following the D-Day invasion, the QUINCY sailed to the Mediterranean to prepare for the invasion of southern France in August of 1944. After her service in the Mediterranean, the cruiser sailed to the US for an overhaul, installation of new equipment, and eventual service in the Pacific. (Floating Drydock)

Shells fired from German shore batteries strike the water just ahead of the QUINCY during the bombardment of Cherbourg, France in June of 1944. The strategic port was bombarded by the QUINCY and other Allied warships in support of US troops advancing up the Cotentin peninsula from the Normandy beachhead. The Germans in Cherbourg surrendered to US troops on 29 June 1944. (US Navy)

The QUINCY's two forward 8-inch gun turrets fire on German positions in southern France on 15 August 1944. The cruiser helped provide fire support for the Allied invasion of southern France (Operation DRAGOON). Propellant powder smoke streamed from the gun barrels soon after firing. An evacuator in each barrel prevented the smoke from entering the turret and overcoming the crewmen inside. (US Navy)

The QUINCY once again cruises the waters of Casco Bay, Maine prior to embarking President Roosevelt for his journey to Malta in January of 1945. Roosevelt met with British Prime Minister Winston Churchill at Malta before they proceeded to Yalta in the Crimea for the 'Big Three' conference with Soviet leader Josef Stalin. In February, the cruiser received President Roosevelt in Egypt's Great Bitter Lake, where he hosted the leaders of Egypt, Ethiopia, and Saudi Arabia. Following her Presidential duties in the Atlantic and Mediterranean, the QUINCY returned to the US for refueling and to take on supplies. She then cruised through the Panama Canal to the Pacific, where she joined the 5th Fleet. (Real War Photos)

The QUINCY stands out of Hampton Roads, Virginia on 5 March 1945. She departed Hampton Roads for the Pacific, via the Panama Canal. Upon her arrival at Pearl Harbor on 20 March, the cruiser joined the 5th Fleet and sailed with Task Force 58 (TF 58) for later strikes on Okinawa and the Japanese home islands. The QUINCY was awarded four Battle Stars for actions in the Pacific during the final seven months of World War Two. (Floating Drydock)

20MM Single Mount

20MM Twin Mount

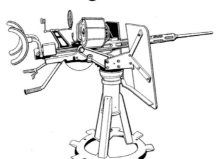

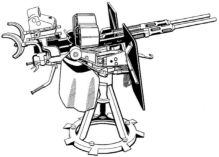

40MM Twin Mount

40MM Quad Mount

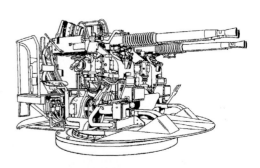

The PITTSBURGH (CA-72) wore a Measure 32/18d camouflage on 9 October 1944, one day before her commissioning. The Measure 32/18d Medium Pattern System was designed to confuse a surface (or subsurface) observer of the cruiser's identity, course, and speed. The PITTSBURGH introduced the single aircraft-handling crane on the fantail to the BALTIMORE class heavy cruisers. Previous ships in the class had two cranes on the fantail. The center-mounted crane forced a modification of the aft 40MM gun battery — two twin mounts versus the previous single quad mount. (Floating Drydock)

The PITTSBURGH lies at anchor while conducting flight operations in the Caribbean on 1 November 1944. One of her two VCS-19 Vought OS2U Kingfisher scout aircraft is spotted on the starboard catapult, which is trained over the side ready for launch. Her other Kingfisher taxied elsewhere in the harbor. PITTSBURGH later departed for the Pacific and reported for duty with Task Group 58.2, formed around the aircraft carrier LEXINGTON (CV-16). She carries an SK-2 air search and SG sea search radar atop her foremast and an SG atop her main mast. (Real War Photos)

The PITTSBURGH stands off the bow of the crippled aircraft carrier FRANKLIN (CV-13), while the light cruiser SANTA FE (CL-60) takes on personnel via a damaged deck edge antenna. The FRANKLIN was damaged by Japanese bombs and torpedoes on 19 March 1945 after her aircraft had struck Kyushu. The PITTSBURGH took the carrier under tow and brought the badly damaged carrier to safety. (Real War Photos)

The PITTSBURGH sailed to Guam minus her bow, but with all hands safe. The teak and steel decking are twisted at the break, but the remainder of the hull was intact and flooding was minimal. Two sailors on the dock looked at the damage in disbelief and wondered how the ship could survive such damage. PITTSBURGH was awarded two Battle Stars for her brief service in the Pacific. (Floating Drydock)

On 4 June 1945 the PITTSBURGH lost 110 feet (33.5 M) of her bow to a Pacific typhoon that produced 70-knot (129.7 KMH) winds and 100-foot (30.5 M) waves. No sailors were lost. The severed bow, dubbed 'McKeesport' for a suburb of Pittsburgh, was recovered and towed to Guam; however, it was not grafted back onto its former location. (Real War Photos)

The PITTSBURGH was fitted with a temporary bow at Guam for her journey to Puget Sound Navy Yard in Bremerton, Washington. She was still undergoing repair and refit when the war in the Pacific ended. She was placed in the reserve fleet after her repairs were completed, but was recalled to active duty when the Korean War began in 1950. (Real War Photos)

The WICHITA (CA-45), camouflaged in Measure 12 with splotches, served in the North Atlantic escorting convoys from America to England in 1942. The camouflage pattern was repeated on the port side. Two Curtiss SOC Seagull aircraft were spotted on her fantail catapults.

Port Camouflage Pattern on the WICHITA

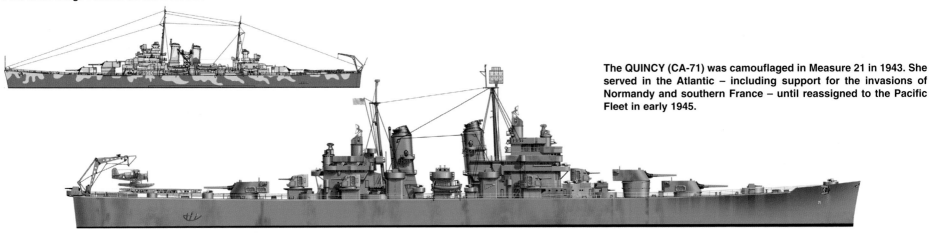

The QUINCY (CA-71) was camouflaged in Measure 21 in 1943. She served in the Atlantic – including support for the invasions of Normandy and southern France – until reassigned to the Pacific Fleet in early 1945.

The CANBERRA (CA-70), camouflaged in Measure 32/18D in late 1944, was named to honor the Australian cruiser HMAS CANBERRA, which was lost at the Battle of Savo Island in 1942. Two OS2U Kingfishers were placed on her catapults.

Port Camouflage Pattern on the CANBERRA

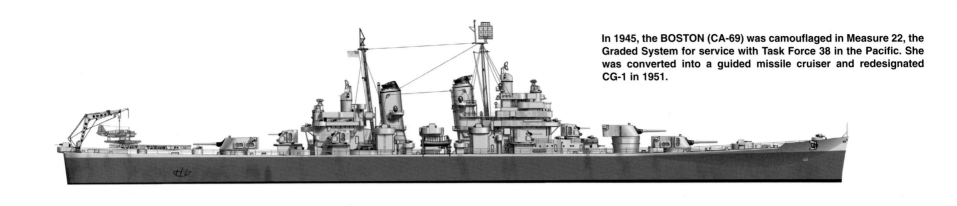

In 1945, the BOSTON (CA-69) was camouflaged in Measure 22, the Graded System for service with Task Force 38 in the Pacific. She was converted into a guided missile cruiser and redesignated CG-1 in 1951.

The OREGON CITY class ROCHESTER (CA-124) was painted in overall Measure 27 for her service off the coast of Korea during the Korean War. The Haze Gray (5-H, FS35237) color scheme is the current standard finish for US Navy surface vessels.

The large cruiser GUAM (CB-2) was camouflaged in Measure 32/7C while serving in the Pacific in early 1945. She and her sister ship ALASKA escorted carrier task forces and conducted shore bombardments during the final months of World War Two. An SC-1 Seahawk was spotted on her port midships catapult.

Starboard Camouflage Pattern on the GUAM

The ST PAUL (CA-73) became the most highly decorated of the BALTIMORE class earning 17 Battle Stars for service during World War Two (one), Korea (eight), and Vietnam (eight). Following commissioning and training she departed for the Pacific where she joined Task Force 38 screening the carrier forces that were conducting air strikes on the Japanese home islands. She is seen here in Measure 21, the Navy Blue System. The cylindrical objects on her stern are smoke generators. (Floating Drydock)

The ST PAUL was extensively modified in the post war period. By May of 1966, her Number One 5-inch turret, all of the 20MM and 40MM mounts, and her two catapults had been removed. She carries an NTDS data link antenna on her forecastle deck and a TACAN antenna at her foremast. Additional antennas, both communications and electronic countermeasures (ECM) crowd the superstructure, stacks, and masts. She was painted in Measure 27, the peacetime Haze Gray (FS35237) scheme. (Floating Drydock)

The ST PAUL fires her forward 8-inch guns at enemy positions at Hungnam, North Korea in December of 1950. The gunfire helped cover the evacuation of United Nations forces and Korean civilians from the port, which was under attack from Communist Chinese forces. The ST PAUL fired the last shot from sea in the Korean War at 2159 hours on 27 July 1953 – one minute before the armistice became effective. (US Navy)

North Vietnamese coastal artillery shells straddle the ST PAUL in the Gulf of Tonkin in August of 1967. The cruiser provided fire support for US and South Vietnamese forces in the north of South Vietnam between 1965 and 1970. She was hit in the bow by a North Vietnamese shell on 2 September 1965; however, there were no casualties. The ST PAUL earned two Meritorious Unit Commendations and the Navy Unit Commendation to go with her eight Battle Stars. (US Navy)

The ST PAUL approaches the port side of the oiler NAVASOTA (AO-106) for an underway replenishment in the Gulf of Tonkin during 1967. The cruiser was fitted with a single sideband (SSB) radio antenna, which rose vertically from the forecastle. A URN-6 TACAN (Tactical Air Navigation) antenna was placed atop the mainmast, with the SPS-37 radar antenna below the URN-6. (Andrew Probert)

Crewmen aboard the NAVASOTA prepare to send cables to the ST PAUL in order to transfer supplies and fuel between the two ships. The oiler's crewmen wear hard hats for head protection while performing their duties. The Mk 54 director for the 8-inch main guns was placed on the rear of the aft superstructure. Forward and above the Mk 54 was the Mk 37 director for the 5-inch secondary weapons. (Andrew Probert)

The ST PAUL's fairly high ride on the water while maneuvering alongside NAVASOTA indicates her lightened condition prior to taking on additional fuel and supplies. The vertical rod attached to the roof of the Number Two 6-inch gun turret was a fixed radio antenna. Her forward 5-inch gunhouse immediately forward of the superstructure was removed during the early 1960s. This modification allowed for additional crew quarters to be placed inside the gunhouse base. Immediately ahead of the aft stack were two ECM (Electronic Countermeasures) antennas. An SPS-8A height finding air search radar antenna was placed atop her aft mast. The ST PAUL completed yearly deployments to the Gulf of Tonkin, off Vietnam, between 1965 and 1970. She served as Pacific Fleet flagship during this period. (Andrew Probert)

Crewmen aboard the ST PAUL fill a cargo net with supplies to transfer to and from the oiler NAVASOTA, which steamed alongside the cruiser during a 1967 replenishment in the Gulf of Tonkin. A 30 foot (9.1 M) motor launch was supported by two davits along the cruiser's starboard side. The breeches of the twin 3-inch (76.2MM) guns were covered with canvas to protect them from corrosive seaspray. Grills at the base of the two stacks reduced the ST PAUL's IR (Infrared) signature. (Andrew Probert)

A cargo net carries spent 8-inch shell propellant casings from the ST PAUL to the NAVASOTA while the two vessels steamed alongside each other. The ammunition casings replaced the separate propellant bags previously used for the 8-inch guns, which allowed for a faster rate of fire. These casings were often dumped overboard, although sometimes they were offloaded for recycling during underway replenishment. The aft fuel line was extended from the NAVASOTA to the ST PAUL's superstructure. (Andrew Probert)

Two seamen aboard NAVASOTA take a breather during refueling of the ST PAUL while both ships were underway in the Gulf of Tonkin during 1967. The oiler extends two fuel lines (fore and aft) to the cruiser's starboard side, where they are fitted to refueling receptacles. The ST PAUL and other OREGON CITY class cruisers held a maximum of 2516.2 tons (2282.7 MT) of fuel oil. The fuel amount gave the vessels a range of 10,000 nautical miles (11,515.2 miles/18,531.3 KM) at a speed of 15 knots (17.3 MPH/27.8 KMH). The ST PAUL's forward Mk 37 5-inch gun director was turned to starboard during the refueling, while the Mk 54 8-inch gun director faced forward. (Andrew Probert)

29

The COLUMBUS conducts her trials in Quincy Bay in June of 1945. She is camouflaged in Measure 21, the Navy Blue System. She carries SG-2 sea search radar atop her main mast and SG sea search and SK-2 air search radar atop her fore mast. She was constructed, like most of the BALTIMORE Class, at Bethlehem Steel, Quincy, Massachusetts. (Floating Drydock)

The HELENA (CA-75) moves slowly through Quincy Bay on 3 September 1945. She is camouflaged in Measure 21, the Navy Blue System. Although completed too late to see service in World War Two, she did see action in the Korean War. The HELENA served as flagship of the Bombardment Task Group early in the conflict. Her performance in Korea earned the cruiser a Presidential Unit Citation of the Republic of Korea and the Korean Service Medal with four stars. (Real War Photos)

The COLUMBUS (CA-74) cruises in the placid waters of Quincy Bay, Massachusetts on the day of her commissioning, 8 June 1945. Following training, she joined the Pacific Fleet off Tsingtao, China. She continued to operate in the Pacific until she was assigned various duties such as flagship to the 6th Fleet in the Mediterranean. In 1959 she began her conversion to a guided missile cruiser. Once completed, COLUMBUS was reclassified CG-12 and became part of the ALBANY class missile cruisers. (Real War Photos)

The OREGON CITY (CA-122) introduced a new single stack design to the BALTIMORE class. Following World War Two, the BALTIMORE class heavy cruisers were split into two separate classes: BALTIMORE (twin stacks) and OREGON CITY (one stack). The OREGON CITY was launched too late to see service in the war, but did serve in the postwar Navy as Flagship of the 4th Fleet in the Atlantic and training Midshipmen from Annapolis. She is camouflaged in Measure 22, the Graded System consisting of a Navy Blue hull and a Haze Gray superstructure. (Floating Drydock)

The OREGON CITY was quickly repainted in Measure 13, Haze Gray in 1946. She carries SK-2 and DBM-I and DBM antennas on the main mast and an SK air search and SG radar atop her foremast. All of her 20MM and 40MM anti-aircraft mounts are covered from the weather. The OREGON CITY was decommissioned in 1947 and spent the next 23 years in mothballs awaiting the call to duty that never came. She was sold and scrapped in 1973. (Floating Drydock)

The ALBANY (CA-123) was commissioned on 15 June 1946 and, after training cruises, joined the 6th Fleet in the Mediterranean where she spent the next ten years operating with US and NATO forces. She carries SG and SK-2 on her maintop and SPS-6B and SG-2 radars on her foretop. The Number One and Two turrets are trained to port following the direction of the MK-34 director. The ALBANY began her conversion to a guided missile cruiser (CG-10) in 1958. (Real War Photos)

The ROCHESTER (CA-124), a member of the OREGON CITY class, was constructed by Bethlehem Steel, Quincy, Massachusetts and launched on 28 August 1945 — too late to see service in World War Two. She was, however, awarded six Battle Stars for her service in Korean War, serving almost continually (except for yard periods) for three years. She is operating here with Task Force 77 off the East Coast of Korea. She mounts an SPS-6B air search radar and an SG-2 surface search radar at her foretop. (Real War Photos)

(Above) The BREMERTON (CA-130) was undergoing experimental work in Casco Bay, Maine on 12 September 1945. What looks like dilapidated paint work or a splotch camouflage scheme is actually her Measure 32 camouflage scheme being changed to Measure 21, Navy Blue. She carries a pair of Curtiss SC-1 Seahawk single seat scout floatplanes on her catapults. She also carries SK air search radar and a URN-3 antenna atop her foremast. THE BREMERTON served with Task Force 77 in Korean waters and earned two Battle Stars for her service. (Real War Photos)

(Left) The FALL RIVER (CA-131) was built by New York Shipbuilding, Camden, New Jersey, launched on 13 August 1944, and commissioned on 1 July 1945, again too late to see service in World War Two. She is camouflaged in Measure 21, Navy Blue. She carries SK-2 and SG radars atop her foremast. The FALL RIVER served as the flagship for Adm F.G. Fahron when he commanded the target vessels for Operation CROSSROADS – the Bikini Atoll atomic bomb tests in 1946. Following the tests, the FALL RIVER was assigned duty as flagship of Cruiser Division 1. The FALL RIVER was decommissioned on 31 October 1947 and stricken on 19 February 1971. (Floating Drydock)

The MACON (CA-132) joined the fleet after the war and was flagship of Cruiser Division 6 (Atlantic) in 1950. By 1951, MACON's 20MM and 40MM anti-aircraft mounts had been removed, twelve 3-inch(7.62 CM)/50 anti-aircraft guns were added, and a helicopter landing pad was mounted on the quarterdeck. A Sikorsky HO3S-1 helicopter, replacing the former float scout planes that occupied the catapults, is lashed onto the pad. The foremast is fitted with SK and SG-2 radars, while SK-2 and SG radar antennas are mounted on the main mast. (Real War Photos)

The TOLEDO (CA-133) was also completed too late to see service in World War Two. Launched on 6 May 1945 and commissioned on 27 October 1946, the TOLEDO served in the Pacific in support of occupation troops in Korea and Japan. When the Korean War broke out in 1950, the TOLEDO made three separate deployments to Korea and earned five Battle Stars. The grills around her stacks were used to reduce the cruiser's infra-red signature. (Real War Photos)

Crewmen load 8-inch shells and propellant powder charges from a lighter (barge) berthed alongside the TOLEDO. Armor piercing (AP) rounds for use against ships weighed 335 pounds (152 KG) each. The wide driving band at the base of each shell conformed to the grooves inside the gun barrel, which increased the projectile's accuracy when fired from the gun. (US Navy)

The LOS ANGELES (CA-135) operates off the Korean coast on 25 August 1951. She was assigned to escort the aircraft carrier BOXER (CV-21) during this period. The cruiser still carried quad 40MM guns, although these were replaced by twin 3-inch guns at her next overhaul in 1952. She was painted in Measure 27, Haze Gray, while her pennant number on the bow was white with black shadowing. The LOS ANGELES made two deployments to Korea and received five Battle Stars for her service. The LOS ANGELES operated as flagship for Admiral Arleigh Burke's Cruiser Division 5 off Korea in 1951. She carried SK-2 and DBM-1 and DBM antennas on her main mast and SPS-6 and an URN antenna on her foremast. (Real War Photos)

The CHICAGO (CA-136), wearing an overall Measure 21 (Navy Blue) scheme, sails to the Pacific in May of 1945. She joined the battleship NORTH CAROLINA (BB-55) and the 3rd Fleet for the final strikes on the Japanese home islands — earning a single Battle Star. A pair of Curtiss SC-1 scouts from VCS-21 are positioned on the two catapults. Her conversion to a guided missile cruiser began in 1958; she was recommissioned as CG-11 on 2 May 1964.

8 Inch (20.3 CM) Mk 12/15 Turret

(BALTIMORE/ OREGON CITY class)

Range Finder Hoods (Port and Starboard)

Gun Gas Vent (4)

8 Inch Mk 16 Mod 0 Turret

(DES MOINES class)

Periscopes

Mk 27 Ranging Radar

The DES MOINES (CA-134) represented the class leader in a new, larger heavy cruiser based on the BALTIMOREs. She is fully dressed out during a port call at Grand Harbour, Valletta, Malta in December of 1951. All of her 40MM guns have been replaced by 12 dual 3-inch/50 anti-aircraft guns. The 8-inch gun Mk 38 directors were placed on raised towers to increase their range. The DES MOINES was painted in Measure 27, a Haze Gray scheme designed for all operating conditions. (Real War Photos)

The SALEM (CA-139) ties up in a Mediterranean port in 1950, accompanied by the submarines ENTEMEDOR (SS-340, outboard) and REQUIN (SSR-481). The SALEM served as 6th Fleet flagship on six separate occasions while deployed to the Mediterranean Sea. The SALEM is now displayed at the US Naval & Shipbuilding Museum in Quincy, Massachusetts – near the Bethlehem Steel yard where she was built. (Real War Photos)

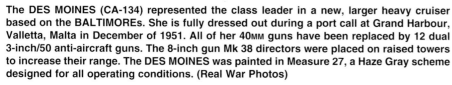

(Above) The SALEM lies anchored at Guantanamo Bay, Cuba on 25 March 1956. Guantanamo Bay was established as a coaling and naval station in 1903. The SALEM was the second of three DES MOINES class heavy cruisers built. She and her two sisters – DES MOINES and NEWPORT NEWS – were 43 feet (13.1 M) longer and 5 feet 8 inches (1.7 M) wider than the earlier BALTIMORE/OREGON CITY Class cruisers. (US Navy)

(Right) The NEWPORT NEWS (CA-148) was the last member of the DES MOINES class and was commissioned on 29 January 1949. She deployed to the Mediterranean on 11 occasions serving with the US 6th Fleet. She was fitted with a Navy Tactical Data System (NTDS) data link antenna on her forecastle and a TACAN (Tactical Air Navigation) antenna atop her foremast in 1962. An SPS-8 antenna was mounted on the main mast and an SK antenna was placed on the foremast. (Real War Photos)

ALASKA Class

The ALASKA class represented a departure from the conventional warship design that had been employed in both US cruisers and battleships of the 1930s and 40s. Some experts speculate that the ALASKAs were the US Navy's answer to the German 27,500 ton (24,948 MT) **SCHARNHORST** class heavy battlecruisers. The SCHARNHORST, and her sister ship **GNEISENAU**, was armed with nine 11 inch (28 cm) guns in three turrets, a secondary battery of twelve 5.91 inch (15 cm) guns paired in six turrets, and was protected by an armor belt ranging from 6.75 inches (17.1 cm) to 13.75 inches (35 cm) thick. Perhaps contributing to the ALASKA's design and construction were reports of a large, new class of heavy cruisers being built in Japan.

Ordered on 9 September 1940, the ALASKA class was originally to consist of six ships: ALASKA (CB-1), **GUAM** (CB-2), **HAWAII** (CB-3), **PHILIPPINES** (CB-4), **PUERTO RICO** (CB-5), and **SAMOA** (CB-6) — all US possessions at the time. Ultimately, only the ALASKA and GUAM were commissioned. The 85% complete HAWAII had her construction suspended in August of 1945 before fitting out could be completed. There was some thought by the Bureau of Shipbuilding (BuShips) to convert the HAWAII into a missile ship and arm her with the US Navy's version of the German V-2 missile, but the plan failed to pass final Congressional approval. The partially completed cruiser was finally scrapped in 1958. The three remaining ALASKA Class cruisers – PHILIPPINES, PUERTO RICO, and SAMOA – were cancelled on 24 June 1943.

The ALASKA was laid down on 17 December 1941, with the GUAM following shortly thereafter on 2 February 1942. Both vessels were built at the New York Shipbuilding yards in

The ALASKA (CB-1) was the lead ship in a new class of 'super heavy cruisers.' They had a gross displacement of 34,260 tons (31,080.7 MT) and mounted nine 12 inch (30.5 CM)/50 naval rifles. The ALASKA was built by New York Shipbuilding, Camden, New Jersey and launched on 15 August 1943. Her original camouflage was Measure 32/1d, a paint scheme originally designed for destroyers operating in the Atlantic. (Real War Photos)

Camden, New Jersey. The ALASKA was commissioned on 17 June 1944 with the GUAM following some three months later.

The ALASKA class cruisers were 808 feet, 6 inches (246.4 M) in overall length, 791 feet, 6 inches (241.2 M) at the waterline, and had a beam of 91 feet (27.7 M). Their draft amounted to 31 feet, 10 inches (9.7 M) and they displaced 29,779 tons (27,015.5 MT) standard and 34,260 tons (31,080.7 MT) full war load. Their size and displacement was equivalent to — and in some cases exceeded — some battleships, leading the US Navy to classify the ships as 'large cruisers.' Most navies of the day would simply have classified the ALASKAs as 'battlecruisers.'

The main machinery spaces housed eight Babcock and Wilcox boilers that produced steam for the four General Electric geared turbines. The ship was able to generate 150,000 horsepower for the four screws. Maximum speed was rated at 33 knots (61.2 KMH). Total fuel bunkerage was 3620 tons (3284 MT) of oil, which provided a range of 12,000 miles (19,312 KM) at 15 knots (27.8 KMH). Eight 850-kilowatt diesel generators were fitted to provide emergency electrical power.

The main battery consisted of nine 12-inch (30.5 cm)/50 caliber Mark 8 guns mounted in three turrets. The main battery turrets followed a conventional layout: two forward and one aft. The guns had a rate of fire of three rounds per minute. The 12-inch guns were capable of firing a 1140 lb (517.1 KG) armor-piercing (AP) round out to a range of 38,573 yards (35,271.2 M) with a muzzle velocity of 2500 feet (762 M) per second. The armor piercing round could penetrate 18 inches (45.7 CM) of armor at a range of 10,000 yards (9144 M). The 12-inch guns were controlled by the Mk 38 director, which provided both optical and radar bearing and range finding.

Her secondary armament consisted of twelve 5-inch/38 (12.7 CM) guns mounted in pairs in six gunhouses — three to port and three to starboard. The 5-inch gun had a range of 37,200 feet (11,338.6 M) when being used as an anti-aircraft weapon, which was almost always the case. The 5-inch rounds could be fitted with a Mk 35 proximity fuse that detonated the round once it came near a target. The 5-inch guns were controlled by the Mk 37 radar gun director. Intermediary anti-aircraft protection amounted to 56 Bofors 40MM cannons employed in 14 quad mounts. These weapons were controlled by the Mk 52 radar gun director. The last resort anti-aircraft weapon was the 20MM Oerlikon cannon. When these 34 guns opened up, the whole crew knew that enemy aircraft had penetrated the 5-inch and 40MM screen.

The ALASKA class cruisers were protected by a nine-inch (22.9 CM) thick armor belt covering the machinery and magazine spaces. The armor was sloped 10° to deflect incoming rounds. The main deck was covered with two sets of armor protection. The outer/upper section

ALASKA Class

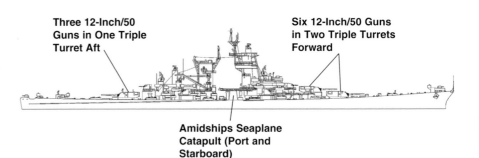

Three 12-Inch/50 Guns in One Triple Turret Aft

Six 12-Inch/50 Guns in Two Triple Turrets Forward

Amidships Seaplane Catapult (Port and Starboard)

was 1.4 inches (3.6 CM) thick and was designed to detonate bombs prematurely, before they penetrated into the ship's vital areas. The inner/lower main deck armor was up to 3.75 inches (9.5 CM) thick. There was no underwater or torpedo protection. The turrets were faced with 12.8-inch (32.5 CM) armor, the roofs with 5 inches (12.7 CM), and the sides with 6 inches (15.2 CM). The turret barbettes were armored with 13 inches (33 CM). The conning tower was armored with up to 10.6 inches (26.9 CM) for protection of the helm and navigation stations. Only 17 percent of the cruisers' weight was devoted to armor protection compared to 40 percent in the battleship **NORTH CAROLINA** (BB-55).

Reverting to the earlier heavy cruiser designs, the aircraft catapults and hangar were placed amidships. This left the quarterdeck free for anti-aircraft guns and their associated directors. Two catapults were fitted, one per side on towers at the deck edge. Two aircraft handling cranes were mounted next to the ship's single stack. These cranes also handled cargo and the ship's boats. The aircraft hangar was located at the base of the conning tower and had a capacity of four aircraft with wings folded. The ALASKA Class were originally equipped with the Vought OS2U Kingfisher in 1944, but were soon equipped with the single seat Curtiss SC-1 Seahawk before the two cruisers were sent to the Pacific.

Following their commissioning and shake down and availability cruises to the Caribbean, the ALASKA and GUAM sailed to the Pacific via the Panama Canal. They joined Task Force 58 (TF-58) — the fast carrier force that brought the fight to the Japanese home islands. The ALASKA and GUAM entered the war in the Pacific in early 1945, and like the BALTIMORE class, arrived too late to engage the depleted Japanese fleet in any surface engagements. They supported the invasions of Iwo Jima and Okinawa and engaged shipping in the East China Sea before striking targets in the Japanese home islands. The two cruisers were primarily used to screen the carrier from *kamikaze* (suicide aircraft) attacks due to their impressive suite of anti-aircraft weapons. Both ships operated with elements of TF-58 and other forces until Japan surrendered on 2 September 1945.

The ALASKA was awarded three Battle Stars and GUAM two Battle Stars for their service in the Pacific during the last year of the Pacific war. Both ships were decommissioned on 17 February 1947 after serving three years on active duty. ALASKA and GUAM were sold and broken up for scrap in the early 1960s.

The ALASKA class cruisers were designed in response to both Germany's 27,500 ton SCHARNHORST and GNEISENAU 'battlecruisers' and reports of a new and larger class of Japanese cruisers. The ALASKA class was faster (33 knots vs 31 knots) and better armed than the German cruisers (12-inch guns vs 11-inch guns). Six ALASKA class cruisers were planned, but only three were built and only two commissioned — ALASKA and her sister GUAM (CB-2). The third, HAWAII (CB-3), was scrapped when she was approximately 85% complete. (Real War Photos)

ALASKA conducts her builder's trials in the Atlantic in early 1944. She carries a pair of Vought OS2U scouts on her two catapults. Her secondary battery consisted of 12 5-inch/38 dual purpose guns in enclosed mounts. The orientation of the 5-inch and 12-inch gun directors and turrets indicates a gunnery exercise is underway. (Real War Photos)

ALASKA continued her workup to final acceptance and commissioning in the Atlantic in 1944. Looking much like a battleship, but with the lean lines of a cruiser, the ALASKA had the gun power and speed to choose her fight. By the time she entered the Pacific; however, her main duties were to provide anti-aircraft cover for the fleet carriers and shore bombardment for the amphibious forces. (Real War Photos)

One of the six 5-inch/38 Mk 32 gunhouses aboard the ALASKA participates in gunnery practice at sea during 1945. The mount captain's sighting station blast hood projected from the aft turret roof section. Flexible bloomers around the gun ports sealed the gunhouse from sea and rainwater. Tracer rounds from the 40MM Bofors cannon streaked towards the aiming point for the 5-inch weapons. (US Navy)

At anchor in 1944, the ALASKA carries an SG sea-search radar at the top of a mast on the stack and SG and SK air-search radars on her foremast atop the tower. Mk 34 fire control directors for the 12- inch guns were mounted on both the conning tower and a tower abaft the single stack. The flagstaff for the US ensign has been moved from the fantail forward to the quarterdeck to allow the fitting of two quad Bofors 40MM anti-aircraft guns. (Real War Photos)

Heavy Cruiser Radars

SK

SK-2

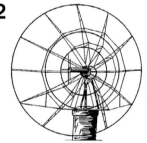

SG

SPS-43

(Above) The ALASKA enters Philadelphia Navy Yard for her post-commissioning fitting out. The small round tubs adjacent to the fantail mounted 40mm guns are shields for the Mk 57 directors. The fantail/quarterdeck area was fitted with four quad 40mm mounts for a total of 16 rapid-fire cannon. Following her post commissioning time, the ALASKA went to the Pacific to join the fleet for the final assault on Japan. (Floating Drydock)

(Below) Before entering the Pacific war, the ALASKA changed her camouflage scheme from Measure 32/1d to Measure 22, the Graded System. She also traded her Vought OS2U Kingfisher scouts for the new Curtiss SC-1 single seat scout on her port catapult. In this configuration, the ALASKA joined TG 58.5 a task group within Task Force 58 – the famed fast carrier task group that would soon be attacking the Japanese home islands. (Elsilrac)

Both the ALASKA and the GUAM were armed with 56 40MM guns in 14 quad mounts and 34 20MM weapons in single and twin mounts. The aircraft-handling crane is swung out to retrieve one of her scout aircraft. Balsa life rafts are mounted on the deck above. (Real War Photos)

The GUAM (CB-2) cruises off Trinidad during her shakedown cruise in December of 1944. She is camouflaged in Measure 32/7c, a scheme that employed three different colors — two grays and black. The GUAM was launched on 12 November 1943 from New York Shipbuilding, Camden, New Jersey and commissioned on 17 September 1944. (Real War Photos)

The ALASKA's 12-inch Mk 8 guns had a range of 38,573 yards (21.9 miles/35.3 KM) when firing an armor piercing Mk 18 shell. The round was capable of penetrating 18 inches (45.7 CM) of armor at 10,000 yards (9144 M), rendering most ship armor useless. The 12-inch guns had a rate of fire of three rounds per minute. (Real War Photos)

The GUAM fires her six forward 12-inch guns broadside during her shakedown cruise in the Caribbean. The Mk 8 turret was unique to the ALASKA class large cruisers. Each main gun turret was electrically powered through hydraulic gear. The gun elevation range was +45° to -3°, with loading performed while the gun was at +7°. The Measure 32/7c camouflage extended to the upper surfaces. (US Navy)

GUAM leaves Philadelphia Navy Yard on 25 October 1944 — one month after her commissioning. Her tall conning tower/mast and tall single stack are silhouetted against the sky and the camouflage is not doing a good job of masking those features. Her Measure 32/7c camouflage was changed to Measure 22, the Graded System, once she entered the Pacific. The Graded System was believed to offer improved camouflage of ships against enemy ships and aircraft in the Pacific. (Floating Drydock)

12 Inch (30.5 CM) Turret

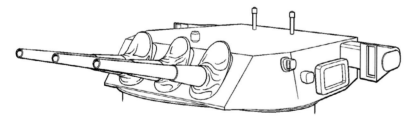

Mk 38 Mod 8 Director

(For the 12 Inch Guns)

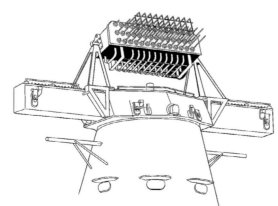

The GUAM cruises off Trinidad, British West Indies while conducting a shakedown cruise in December of 1944. By early 1945, she was screening Task Force 58 off Japan. Atop her main tower mast is a Mk 38 radar controlled director for her 12-inch guns. Another Mk 38 director was fitted to the top of a tower aft of the single stack. (Real War Photos)

The GUAM lies at anchor somewhere in the Atlantic in early 1945. Her Measure 32/7c camouflage paint scheme is already showing the wear and tear caused by months at sea. The low stern and high bow sheer, combined with the dazzle pattern camouflage, made the GUAM appear to be sinking at the stern. Her main yards are dressed for some occasion.

The GUAM was decommissioned on 17 February 1947, no longer needed in the post-war US Navy. She was placed in the reserve fleet where she remained until sold for scrap on 24 May 1961. The GUAM earned two Battle Stars for her brief service in the Pacific. The GUAM served as the Flagship of Cruiser Task Force 95, which also included her sister the ALASKA. (Elsilrac)

The Number One gun in the Number Three turret is elevated, while guns Two and Three are set at 7° for loading. The 5-inch gunhouse immediately forward of the Number Three turret was turned to starboard and the two guns are elevated at a high angle. (Floating Drydock)

An aircraft machinist mate sits on the float of his charge, a Curtiss SOC Seagull scout aircraft. The SOC, along with the Vought OS2U Kingfisher, was a standard floatplane for the US Navy from 1937 until 1945. Both aircraft began being replaced by the Curtiss SC-1 Seahawk in 1945. The Seagull carried a crew of two: a pilot and a gunner/radioman. The SOC could also carry two 250-pound (113.4 KG) bombs and was armed with two 0.30 caliber (7.62MM) machine guns. (Real War Photos)

Heavy Cruiser Scout Aircraft, 1939-1950

Curtiss SOC Seagull

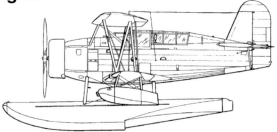

Vought-Sikorsky OS2U Kingfisher

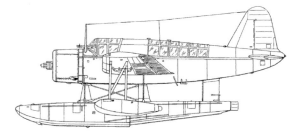

Curtiss SC Seahawk

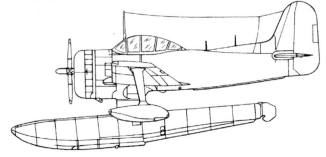

Sikorsky HO3S

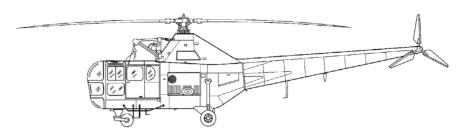

The Vought-Sikorsky OS2U Kingfisher was operational on all US heavy cruisers during World War Two. This Kingfisher is launched from a ship's catapult, while its pilot and gunner/radioman are braced for the sudden acceleration. Scout aircraft were responsible for spotting gunfire for the ship, search and rescue, and general liaison duties for the cruisers. Each US heavy cruiser normally carried four aircraft. (Real War Photos)

The Curtiss SC-1 Seahawk was designed to replace both the SOC and the OS2U on the decks of all US battleships and cruisers. The Seahawk was a single seat floatplane and was armed with two wing-mounted 0.50 caliber (12.7MM) machine guns. The aircraft had a top speed of 313 MPH (503.7 KMH). This SC-1 was hoisted aboard the ALASKA in 1945. (Real War Photos)

Conversions

In 1951, during the height of the Korean War, the US Navy took the first step into the missile age by beginning the conversion of the **BOSTON** (CA-69) into a guided missile cruiser. The BOSTON was soon followed by the **CANBERRA** (CA-70) in 1952.

The conversion of the BOSTON and CANBERRA included the removal of the Number Three 8-inch turret and the Number Five 5-inch turret and utilizing these areas for the installation of a pair of **SAM-N-7** (later **RIM-2**) **Terrier** missile launchers. The launchers were mounted on two levels with the spaces under the launchers and the former aircraft hangar converted into missile magazines. The Terrier missiles had to be stored vertically and kept cool.

The Terrier had a speed of over Mach 2.5 and a range of over 35 miles (56.3 KM). The Terrier was normally fitted with a high explosive (HE) warhead, but a one kiloton W-45-0 nuclear warhead could also be used. The beam-riding, semi-active homing missiles were guided using the two antennas of the Mk 25 Mod 7 radar system — one for range and bearing, and another for altitude determination. The missile was equipped with solid fuel booster and sustainer motors.

These conversions were completed by 1956. BOSTON, the class leader, was recommissioned under the designation CG-1, while the CANBERRA was designated CG-2. Both vessels were assigned to Cruiser Division Six (CRUDIV-6) for operations in the Atlantic with occasional deployments to the US 6th Fleet in the Mediterranean. Both ships eventually found their way to Vietnamese coast where they conducted off-shore fire support for operations on land.

Following the success of the BOSTON and CANBERRA conversions, the **ALBANY** (CA-123 and class leader), **CHICAGO** (CA-136), and **COLUMBUS** (CA-74) began their more extensive conversions beginning over the course of 1957-1958. The work included stripping

The BOSTON (CAG-1, ex CAG-10), was the ex-CA-69 that was converted to a guided missile cruiser. The aft turret was removed and replaced by a pair of RIM-2 Terrier missile launchers mounted on the extended aft superstructure. The aircraft hanger and adjoining spaces were converted into missile storage and maintenance facilities. Additionally, a Mk 25 Mod 7 guidance radar system was installed to determine range, bearing, and altitude of the targets for the Terrier missiles. (Floating Drydock)

the entire superstructure from the deck up and replacing it with a modern shape never seen on any other warship. Unlike the two earlier conversions that retained most of their guns, the ALBANY class were all missile cruisers — with the exception of a pair of open-mount 5-inch/38 anti-aircraft guns installed at the insistence of President John F. Kennedy.

The ALBANY class conversion included the installation of a single **RIM-8 Talos** twin missile launcher, one fore and aft on the centerline of the ship, and a twin **RIM-24 Tartar** missile launcher on each side of the conning tower.

The Talos surface-to-air missile (SAM) was 38 feet (11.6 M) long and had a speed on target of over Mach 2.5. The missile could be armed with a 465 pound (210.9 KG) high explosive (HE) warhead or a five kiloton W-30 nuclear warhead. Talos had a range of over 60 nautical miles (69.1 miles/111.2 KM) and could also be used in the surface-to-surface role. The missile employed a solid rocket booster and a ramjet sustainer motor. Talos used both beam riding and semi-active terminal homing to close on the target.

The Tartar missile system was used for close-in anti-aircraft defense and had a length of 15 feet (4.57 M), a range of over 40 miles (64.4 KM), and a speed of Mach 2.5. The missile employed semi-active homing and was equipped with a high explosive warhead. Throughout their service lives, the Terrier, Talos, and Tartar missiles were subjected to a continuing series of improvements. These upgrades were in terms of range, speed, target acquisition, and electronic countermeasures discrimination (the ability to see through jamming or interference from the target).

A triple tube Mk 32 torpedo launcher was placed on the main deck on each side of the forward superstructure. The Mk 32 launcher was used for the nuclear-tipped **UUM-44 SUBROC** (Submarine Rocket) anti-submarine torpedo. Once launched, the ship would go to full power in the opposite direction from the launch point to escape the torpedo's blast effects. An eight-cell **RUR-5 ASROC** (Anti-Submarine Rocket) missile launcher was placed amidships. This position was originally allocated for a **RGM-15 Regulus II** cruise missile launcher; however, the ASROC was deemed a more effective weapon system.

BOSTON Class CAG

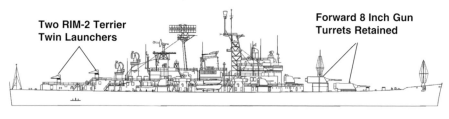

Two RIM-2 Terrier Twin Launchers

Forward 8 Inch Gun Turrets Retained

ALBANY Class CG

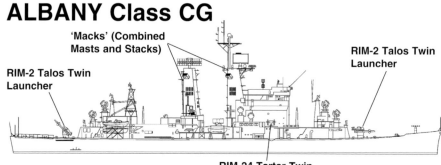

'Macks' (Combined Masts and Stacks)

RIM-2 Talos Twin Launcher

RIM-2 Talos Twin Launcher

RIM-24 Tartar Twin Launcher

The CHICAGO served off North Vietnam hitting radar installations with a special anti-radar version of the Talos (RGM-8H) missile and, on one occasion, MiGs (Mikoyan-Gurevich fighters) that were preparing to attack a US Navy aircraft engaged in mining Haiphong Harbor. On 9 May 1972, CHICAGO fired at least one Talos missile at a range of 48 miles (77.2 км), destroying one of the MiGs. The remaining North Vietnamese Air Force MiGs fled the area.

The COLUMBUS was decommissioned in 1975 and later scrapped. The ALBANY and the CHICAGO soldiered on, perhaps due to their improved command and control facilities, until 1980 when they were decommissioned and placed in reserve.

The second conversion undertaken on a BALTIMORE class cruiser was on the **NORTHAMPTON** (CA-125). She was laid down at Bethlehem Steel in Quincy, Massachusetts on 31 August 1944. The NORTHAMPTON was cancelled on the builder's ways when approximately 60 percent complete. She was reordered on 1 July 1948 as a Task Force Command Ship and designated CLC-1. Historically, cruisers and battleships were utilized by flag officers and their staffs as flagships for fleet operations. The NORTHAMPTON was configured for use by fast carrier commanders and had an elaborate antenna array and a Combat Information Center (CIC). She was built with an additional deck level over the main deck and had flag accommodations for 450 staff personnel and a ship's complement of over 1200 officers and enlisted men. The NORTHAMPTON was redesignated a command ship (CC-1) and made available to national authorities for use by the Executive Branch of the US Government in 1961. She was to be used as a floating command post in the event of a nuclear attack on the United States.

The NORTHAMPTON was originally armed with four 5-inch (12.7 см)/54 Mk 16 single mounts and eight 3-inch (7.62 см)/50 in twin mounts. All of the guns, with the exception of one 5-inch, were removed in 1962. A helicopter deck was positioned on the quarterdeck, but no hangar facilities were provided.

The NORTHAMPTON was fitted with one of the largest radar antennas to go to sea in the form of the diamond-shaped SPS-2 air-search antenna. The SPS-2 radar was beached in 1962 along with most of her armament. A Navy Tactical Data System (NTDS) and tropospheric scatter antennas, as well as SPS-37 and SPS-8A antennas, were mounted on the deck and masts.

The NORTHAMPTON served as the Flagship of the 6th Fleet from 1954 to 1955 in the Mediterranean and Flagship of the 2nd Fleet in the Western Atlantic from 1955 to 1961. A decision to use aircraft for the National Command role was made in the early 1970s; consequently, the NORTHAMPTON was decommissioned and put into reserve.

The BOSTON has her missile launchers fully armed and in the ready to fire position. Eight 3-inch, radar controlled, automatic guns in twin mounts replaced the 12 40MM cannons that had been standard for World War Two operations. She retained five of her six 5-inch mounts; the number six mount was beached to provide space for the Mk 27 radar antennas. The Terrier missiles had to be stored vertically and kept cold to preserve their guidance capability. (Floating Drydock)

The ALBANY (CG-10, ex-CA-123) was the first US all-missile cruiser. She was armed with two twin RIM-8 Talos missile launchers and two twin RIM-24 Tartar missile launchers, plus RUR-5 ASROC and UUM-44 SUBROC launchers. The twin tower 'macks' (a combination of stack and mast) provided platforms for the radar antennas and diffused the exhaust gases. The deck between the aft mack and the tower for the SPS-30 radar was to be used for a RGM-15 Regulus II surface-to-surface missile launcher. (Floating Drydock)

NORTHAMPTON Class CC

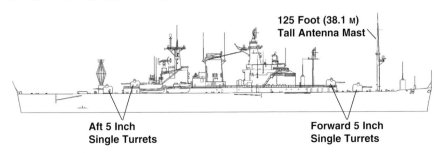

125 Foot (38.1 м)
Tall Antenna Mast

Aft 5 Inch
Single Turrets

Forward 5 Inch
Single Turrets

The extensively modified ALBANY was festooned with various antennas in 1974. The antenna on the bow above the pennant number served the Naval Tactical Data System (NTDS), a radio network which provided target information to other fleet warships. Immediately aft and above the Talos launcher were two large SPG-49 tracking radar antennas. Above and below the SPG-49s were smaller SPW-2 radar antennas for providing mid-course guidance to the missiles. The SPS-43 air-search radar antenna was mounted atop the aft mack. (Floating Drydock)

The COLUMBUS (CG-12, ex-CAG-12, ex-CA-74) was the second in a class of all missile cruisers commissioned during the early 1960s. Like her two sisters, she was armed with Talos missile launchers fore and aft and Tartar missile launchers port and starboard of the bridge superstructure. The two large SPG-49 tracking antennas were augmented by the smaller SPW-2 mid-course correction antennas above and below the main arrays. The ship was not yet fitted with both the SPS-30 height finding radar antennas for atop the bridge and aft lower mast and the midships 5-inch/38 guns. (Floating Drydock)

Guided Missiles and Launchers

RIM-2 Terrier Missile   Terrier Launcher   RIM-24 Tartar Missile   Tartar Launcher   RIM-8 Talos Missile   Talos Launcher

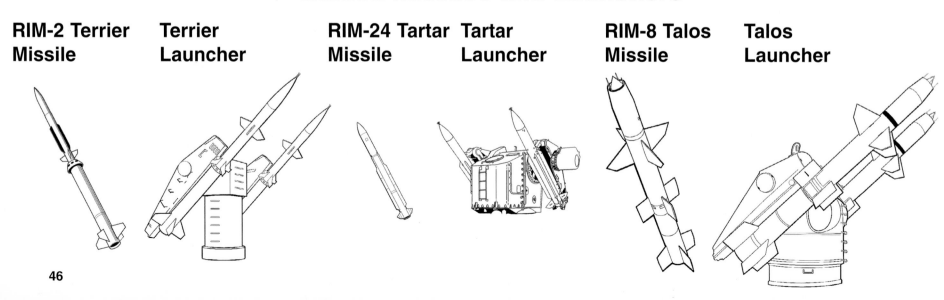

The ALBANY's SPS-30 height finding radar antenna was mounted atop her bridge superstructure. The starboard Tartar missile launcher was located on the next deck level up from the main deck, while farther up and aft were two SPG-51 tracking and illumination radar antennas for the Tartar missiles. A three-tube UUM-44 SUBROC launcher was mounted on the main deck adjacent to the Tartar missile structure. (Floating Drydock)

ALBANY and her sisters were equipped with an eight-tube RUR-5 ASROC missile launcher box amidships, and 5-inch/38 single mounts port and starboard. The gun's Mk 56 radar director was mounted on a platform above the gun. The grilles on the mack diffused and cooled the engineering exhaust gases, which reduced the ship's infrared signature. The mack top was fitted with an SPS-43 air search radar antenna. (Floating Drydock)

The CANBERRA (CG-2) was berthed for inclining tests at New York Shipbuilding in Camden, New Jersey on 5 May 1956. A Mk 34 director for the 8-inch guns was mounted atop the bridge, while the Mk 37 5-inch gun director mounted aft of the Mk 34 was fitted with a Mk 28 radar antenna dish. An SPS-8 air-search radar antenna was mounted atop the tower foremast. Her armor belt, protecting the engineering spaces, was at the midships waterline. (Floating Drydock)

Automatic 3-inch/50 anti-aircraft guns replaced the CANBERRA's 40MM guns of World War Two. Four ready round ammunition lockers were mounted next to the guns. The two ship's boats are a 33-foot (10.1 M) Mk 2 personnel boat – believed to be the captain's gig – placed above a 33-foot Mk 2 utility boat. The stack was fitted with grilles to help cool the exhaust gases. (Floating Drydock)

The CANBERRA and the BOSTON retained their forward 8-inch turrets and midships 5-inch/38 mounts. One of six Mk 63 directors was mounted above the port forward 5-inch mount. The Mk 63 could be interfaced with the Mk 34 air-search radar to provide precise tracking of aerial targets for the 5-inch and 3-inch guns. The CANBERRA underwent inclining tests at New York Shipbuilding in 1956. An additional 60,000 pounds (27,216 KG) of ballast was placed on the forecastle deck for inclining the ship. (Floating Drydock)

The addition of twin Terrier missile launchers and the lower Mk 25 radar antenna, along with the extension of the aft superstructure, eliminated any space for aircraft, catapults, and cranes. The vertically stored missiles were elevated from below deck directly onto the launcher arms. The CANBERRA's port quarterdeck had 60,000 pounds of ballast placed on it during inclining tests on 5 May 1956. (Floating Drydock)

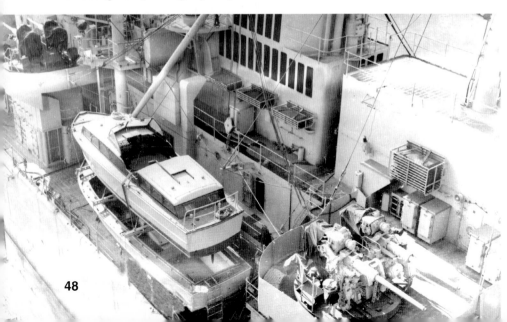

The NORTHAMPTON (CC-1, ex CA-125) was designed as a Command and Control ship to be used as a floating base for flag officers in case of a national emergency. In 1961, she was converted to a National Emergency Command Post Afloat (NECPA) for use by the President and his advisors in case of a nuclear attack on the United States. The NORTHAMPTON was built with an additional deck atop the main deck to accommodate the additional personnel required to operate the ship. She was armed with four 5-inch/54

Mk 16 guns offset from the ship's centerline – two guns forward, two guns aft. A 125 foot (38.1 M) tall antenna mast was placed ahead of the forward 5-inch turret. Smaller vertical antennas for broadband radios were placed on the fore and aft decks. A parabolic antenna – believed to receive satellite transmissions – was mounted atop the foremast. An SPS-37 air search radar antenna was fitted to the mainmast, with an SPS-8A height finder radar antenna above and behind it. (Elsilrac)

More US Warship Books

4004 US Battleships, Part 2

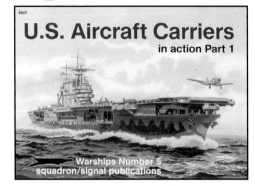

4005 US Aircraft Carriers

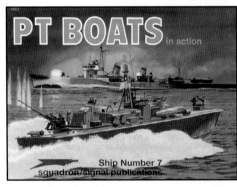

4007 PT Boats

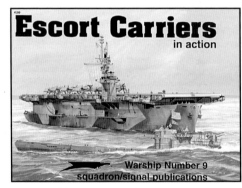

4009 Escort Carriers

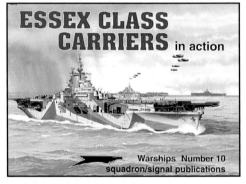

4010 Essex Class Carriers

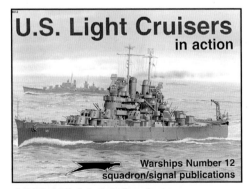

4012 US Light Cruisers

4014 US Heavy Cruisers, Pt 1

from squadron/signal publications